# THE CONTRACTORS GUIDE TO INSURANCE

## Matthew J. Rogers, CRIS

ANSWERS YOUR QUESTIONS REGARDING INSURANCE,
BONDING, CLAIMS AND WORKERS' COMPENSATION

# CONTENTS

# CHAPTER 1
## COMMERCIAL INSURANCE

**Commercial Insurance is an essential part of all construction projects!**

The primary purpose of construction insurance is to protect your clients against the risk created during and after a construction job has been completed. Construction insurance is in the category of commercial Insurance, not personal insurance. It is essential to recognize the difference between these two types of insurance.

Commercial insurance is usually purchased to generate income for the insured (the contractor or business that bought the policy), as in a construction business. When new contractors start their businesses, they often approach buying commercial insurance the same way they would when purchasing personal insurance. There is a **BIG** difference in purchasing auto, health, or life insurance; these types of insurance are not even similar to commercial insurance.

Quite often, when buying personal insurance, price is the sole consideration. You purchase auto insurance, for example, and usually never really see or talk with your agent.

The only time you have any agent contact is when you wish to make a change or file a claim after an incident has happened. Commercial insurance is different from personal insurance in that it is not one-size-fits-all. As your business grows and develops, so do your insurance needs. For this reason, when seeking commercial insurance, it is crucial to consider coverage and service, in addition to the price.

Your broker will be a partner, so you need to select someone to handle your commercial insurance needs with which you can develop a strong, trusting relationship. It is essential to have the proper coverage before beginning a job. Contractors can purchase four main types of insurance policies to help protect their company and customers if a claim is filed.

**The four main types of insurance that contractors buy are:**

1. **General Liability insurance**
2. **Worker's Compensation insurance**
3. **Commercial Auto insurance**
4. **Excess/Umbrella insurance**

The following chapters will include each type of insurance and provide pertinent examples of why  commercial insurance is essential and used when necessary.

# CHAPTER 2
## GENERAL LIABILITY INSURANCE

The first type of insurance that most contractors are requested to have is general liability. General liability insurance is in place to protect liabilities the contractor may create while working on the job or after the job is completed.

There are diverse types of contracts on which an insurance policy can be written, and not all policies are created equally. There are *two types of general liability policies* that you should know about when buying insurance for your company:

**The first type** of general liability insurance is a surplus line or non-admitted policy. Non-admitted policies are *not* regulated by the insurance department in the state of coverage.

**The second type** of general liability insurance is an admitted policy. Your state's department of insurance regulates admitted policies.

What does that mean for you, the insured? There is a lot to say about **surplus line** or **non-admitted policies**. The surplus line/non-admitted policies have a lower cost. However, the coverage may exclude things that reflect the lower price.

The other thing to know about surplus line or non-admitted policies is that if you work on governmental jobs in a city, municipality, or state, they may only accept admitted policies. When you receive the job's insurance requirements, it will usually explain how much coverage they desire, what rating they want the insurance company to have, and if they only want admitted insurance.

I have often seen a city, municipality, or state accept a  surplus line/non-admitted policy *if* the carrier or insurance company has an **A- XII** rating or better. So, don't assume that city, municipalities, or state jobs will only accept admitted policies.

Another important note with regard to surplus line/non-admitted policies is that just because a policy is non-admitted doesn't *always* mean the coverage is less than an admitted policy. It depends on the contract on which the policy is written. Therefore, I advise you to read your policy and speak to a professional commercial insurance broker. Knowing your policy is essential if you don't need specific coverage and added expense.

There are also instances when your state doesn't offer coverage for your trade. For example, residential plumbers (high-risk trade) can have difficulty finding an admitted policy in California.

This is likely due to the prevalence of claims for residential plumbing work, which makes it harder for the insurance company to take on the risk. Some companies do take plumbers but mostly on surplus/non-admitted policies. Other examples of high-risk trades which are often, though not always, on surplus/non-admitted policies are roofers, tree trimmers, demolition, fire sprinkler installation, waterproofing, plaster/stucco, and welders.

Many of the insurance companies have different companies under their umbrella. So often, the policy you buy may have been written by an affiliate of a much larger insurance company that owns them. I mention this because sometimes contractors are unsure if they are with a quality company since they are unfamiliar with the name.

Larger, well-established financial groups often back these companies. Always talk to your broker to learn more about your policy and the company behind it. This will give you confidence in your insurance coverage. Be advised that some insurance companies will sell both surplus/non-admitted **and** admitted insurance policies for the same exposure but under different names.

This information is necessary for you to be aware of since it supports the idea that the surplus/non-admitted insurance may not be less coverage. This is an

**HONESTY.**
**INTEGRITY.**
**TRUST.**

example of why it is essential to familiarize yourself with your policy and create a trusting partnership with your broker.

When you purchase a surplus/non-admitted policy, you will be asked to sign a document informing you it is a surplus line/non-admitted policy. Admitted Insurance is what your agent should try to sell you if there is an option. Admitted Insurance means that the rates and the policy have been approved by the state for which the coverage has been purchased.

When this happens, it means the department of insurance may assist you in that state if there is an issue with paying a claim or if the company becomes insolvent. When buying general liability, many contractors will ask if they can save money by buying less coverage.

For example, if you buy $1,000,000 coverage instead of $2,000,000, would you save money on the premium? The

9

answer is that most of the time, the amount of coverage isn't what determines the majority of the premium/cost of the policy.

Most General Liability policies premiums are being configured by:

1. **Roughly 1% of the gross receipts for your business.**
2. **Your cost of subcontractors hired.**
3. **Employee payroll.**

The three elements above inform the insurance underwriter regarding the level of exposure you have in the event of a claim. The more business you do, the more subcontractors you hire, the more risk you incur, and the more employees you have working in the field, the higher the chances are you'll file a claim.

The primary reason for this is that the person who hires the subcontractor (you) is more likely to be responsible for a problem that a subcontractor might create since they will have more interest in the work than someone doing one part of many jobs on a project.

For this reason, many insurance companies don't want the insured (you, the contractor) to subcontract out more than 50% of the work. Another issue with subcontractors is that sometimes it's hard to know who created a problem. Should something go wrong on a job, people often point fingers.

As a result, it's often the case when there is a claim or lawsuit on a project, all contractors and subcontractors get sued. General liability insurance is critically important to have in these types of claims. In life, there is only so much we can anticipate.

It would help if you had insurance for things you can't even imagine.

**Here are a few examples:**

This example involved a lawsuit by a renter against his landlord for ten million dollars for a hole in his ceiling that he claimed was giving him health issues. A client of mine who is a painter went to an apartment to provide a quote to paint the unit's interior. He didn't know about any of the ongoing issues or pending lawsuits.

The painter took photos of the apartment and gave the landlord a quote to paint it. Ultimately, my client never did any work yet was later brought into this existing lawsuit for a job he never even did. For some reason, the landlord named my client in the lawsuit. We still don't know how or why.

The painter's general liability insurance paid approximately $20,000 on this claim, probably because they realized my client was not at all in the wrong and just wanted to settle and get away from this bizarre situation. This is not an isolated claims incident but another situation that occurs often. It is essential to have insurance and a knowledgeable broker to consult should the unexpected occur.

In another example regarding a general liability claim, a drywall contractor was working on the 15th floor of a high-rise condominium building. Most units in the building were valued at over a million dollars.

The owner told him that the work needed to be done as quickly as possible. The contractor replaced the drywall and used a heat gun to help dry the plaster. While doing this, one of the fire sprinklers went off for about five minutes doing damage to the unit and two more below. The claims adjuster looked at the issue and noticed that the manufacturer of these particular sprinklers was known for having malfunctions.

The drywall contractor claimed he never went near the sprinkler with the heat gun, and he was on the other side of the room from the sprinkler. However, the insurance company paid around $500,000 for this claim. The experienced drywall contractor didn't feel it was his fault and was angry when his insurance premium increased. In his frustration, he missed a crucial point. His insurance did its job and saved him from financial ruin.

This example of a general liability claim involved an incident when a tree-trimmer accidentally dropped a tree branch on the neighbor's BBQ next door to the tree trimming house. The grill owner was upset and had difficulty assessing the damage and how much it would cost to replace the lid.

The contractor was happy to make a claim on his policy to help deal with the issue, given the fact that the neighbor was looking to benefit as much as possible financially. The insurance company specializes in dealing with this type of situation. The claim was made on the contractor's general liability policy.

The claims adjuster met with the grill owner, and the claim was dropped. I'm sure the claims adjuster explained the penalties for insurance fraud to the grill owner, and he realized  it was not a wise path to go down. This is another instance when having Insurance can save you from having a more expensive problem.

A contractor was working on a house when he accidentally broke a window awning in a similar situation. The homeowner was upset and was sure that the house must have structural damage since the awning was knocked down. The homeowner wanted to remove part of his roof and hire an engineer to look under the roof and ensure no structural damage.

The contractor was willing to pay for all of this by making payments to the homeowner, but the homeowner was concerned that the contractor could not make payments and did not accept this solution. The contractor then filed a claim under his general liability insurance, and the claims adjuster met with the homeowner, and the claim was dropped.

As you can see from these examples, sometimes insurance can protect you without too much effort. Just the protection of having an insurance company involved in a possible fraudulent or inaccurate claim can make a problem go away a lot easier and very effectively.

**The Sunset Clause** – This is fundamental information regarding a General Liability policy. There is what is called a Sunset Provision or Sunset Clause on many policies, which refers to the fact that the coverage stops covering the work 3-5 years after

what are other words for sunset provision?

sunset regulation, phase-out, phase-out regulation, phase-out arrangements

completion. Policies that don't have the Sunset Provision/Clause will cover the work ten years after the work has been completed since the statute of limitations law runs out.

Sunset Provisions leave contractors in a dangerous position, which is why I do not recommend them to my clients. Most claims on construction jobs happen between years 6 and 8. When these claims happen, everyone who worked on the job usually gets brought into the claim, even if their trade wasn't part of the issue. That's why it's necessary to read your policy carefully and talk with your broker to ensure that your work is covered long after it has been completed.

It is ideal to keep the same policy year after year to help protect any prior years' work and ensure no coverage gap. It is

easier for the insurance company to take on the claim when there aren't any "grey areas" regarding which policy was in place when the work was completed.

The insurance company can verify that clear coverage with a consistent policy was in place. There are times when another might replace one policy. For instance, sometimes the insurance company may not be selling the coverage you need anymore, or another company comes along with better coverage and lower pricing. It is crucial to understand that there are risks to changing policies, and you need to be informed to prevent an issue down the line.

For instance, while some policies will pick up the prior work on which you still have coverage, many policies do not. You can lose the previous year of insurance by changing your policy. It is something you should know about before moving your policy somewhere else. It is essential that you discuss it with your broker to avoid issues with your coverage.

The most common reason to change policies is when you begin with a minor policy for your business and outgrow it as your business expands and becomes more profitable. Usually, this happens when you go from working with homeowners to working on commercial jobs. Homeowners are typically less informed about the type of insurance you have if they even inquire at all.

Commercial businesses are more educated regarding types of insurance. The homeowner is usually simply happy you have insurance at all. When you start getting bigger jobs for larger companies, they will usually have a sample insurance requirement they will send you.

That is when you (the contractor) will email the requirements to your broker and ask, "What does this mean?" Or "Can you help me with this insurance?" Remember that your professional insurance broker is available to help navigate your insurance needs as your business evolves. Some other situations involve increasing coverage or purchasing a new policy that meets your customer's requirements to acquire the job or work as a subcontractor and needs to fulfill the general contractor's insurance requirements.

If you'd like to be considered to bid on jobs for cities, municipalities, schools, and larger institutions, you will need to be registered by that organization to be on their bid list. When you sign up to be on a bid list, you will need to have the required insurance active before bidding on these types of jobs.

I recommend that you give the requirements to your broker or agent, so they can make sure the insurance you buy will be accepted by the company requesting it. You don't want to purchase a policy and assume it will satisfy all requirements. Sometimes, the company requesting insurance will have specific limits to distinct types of coverage and require a top-rated insurance company. If you purchase an unacceptable policy, you might have to cancel it and lose money.

Many people think that most policies are the same if the coverage amount is equal, but this is not always true. I would always ask your broker to ensure you are getting the correct policy for the job.

**AUTHOR'S NOTE;**

This chapter was written to provide you with an overview of general liability insurance. I could quickly write an entire book on understanding general liability insurance for contractors. However, I believe this chapter will contain information regarding what to look for and what questions are relevant to ask your broker or agent when acquiring a general liability policy.

# CHAPTER 3
## WARRANTY VS GENERAL LIABILITY

I t is essential to understand that your general liability insurance is designed to protect you and your business if your client sustains ***bodily injury or property damage*** from your work. Therefore, if an issue arises on the job and there has been damage to the property or injury to the client, you may be held personally responsible for making things right. **Liability insurance is a must!**

Furthermore, liability policies contain "exclusions" or situations that do not qualify for coverage. What is and isn't covered by your general liability insurance is not quickly answered. However, every policy is unique, as are the circumstances of every claim.

You must talk with your broker about the exact nature of the type of work you will be doing so that they can ensure that an appropriate policy is tailored to meet your needs.

Recently, I saw a claim for a contractor who was doing work at a veterinary clinic. The contractor unplugged a refrigerator to do work around it.

He left for the weekend and forgot to plug it back in. This resulted in $12,000 in medication spoiling. The question is, is there exclusion in this contractor's policy for appliances? If so, he will have to cover the cost of the lost medication himself.

After the issue is resolved, the contractor will either remember to check a refrigerator before unplugging it or require that a client have everything removed before doing the work to manage the risk of liability. In another instance, a contractor was awarded a project to install windows in a new townhome community.

This was his first new construction job, and he began the project without checking in with his broker to ensure his work would be covered. After the job, water damage was sustained to the building due to the faulty installation of the windows. This sounds like a claim that would be covered, as there was apparent damage to the property.

However, the contractor's claim was denied since his original policy was excluded for new townhomes. When the policy was purchased, the contractor stated that he did not do this type of work. In sharing the above examples, I hope to stress a significant point that will protect your company and your clients in the  long run. You need to approach your work with a risk management mindset.

Whenever you are awarded a job, you should take the time to contact your broker. You need to discuss the nature of the work you are about to do and allow them to work with you to ensure that your current coverage meets your needs.

Contractors' insurance needs to evolve with you as your business grows and changes. Policies can always be adjusted along the way to keep up with you and your growth. This is yet another reason why commercial insurance is different from personal insurance. You need to have regular touchpoints with your broker, who should ideally specialize in construction, to ensure your coverage is up to speed.

**Contractor's Warranty** - Often, contractors offer a contractor's warranty for the first year of a job, which means they will deal with any issues that may arise and fix them. Insurance is available if this is not a possibility or the damages  are too great or expensive for a contractor to cover. Remember, insurance is a safety net for your client.

It's good to keep in mind, though, if you decide to handle an issue on your own and not notify your insurance company, you will most likely void your insurance coverage for that job or problem. For example, a prime contractor gave his floor contractor flooring material to install near a pool; however, the product was not meant to be installed near water.

The prime contractor realized this after the flooring was installed. He raced to replace the flooring to make the homeowner happy. After fixing the issue himself under the contractor's warranty, he filed a claim.

This claim was denied because the insurance company could not verify the issue since the problem had already been resolved. Always consult your broker or agent if you have a problem and are uncertain if something is a contractor's warranty issue or a general liability claim. Insurance is typically designed to fix the problem, not reimburse the contractor.

There have been cases where someone's attorney steps in before their insurance company is involved, and it should have been a general liability claim. In turn, the case is mismanaged because the attorney is usually not an insurance expert. Most policies state that if a third party enters negotiations, that is grounds for voiding the policy.

If the insurance company does decide to pay the claim, it often costs them more money since they were not the initial contact. Make sure something is a manageable contractor's warranty issue before you complicate a situation since this could negatively affect your rates and credibility to be insured.

# CHAPTER 4
## WORKERS' COMPENSATION

Workers' compensation insurance protects your employee if they get injured on the job. This type of insurance can be the most expensive cost a contractor incurs, especially if they're doing

business in California. The high price of worker's compensation in California is that the laws have been written to protect employees and the cost of medical care.

The California Worker's Compensation Insurance Rating Bureau (WCIRB) creates the classification codes and issues Experience Modification Ratings (XMOD). An XMOD rating is given to all companies that purchase worker's compensation insurance. This rating reflects a company's claim history.

If a company has too many claims, they will have a poor  XMOD and vice versa for those with few claims. A poor XMOD corresponds to higher rates, which may negatively impact a company's ability to stay competitive. WCIRB gives each job or business type the classification or "class" code, reflecting its exposure. Some classification codes in California issue a dual wage code for the same job. The following is an example of how the classification works.

If the worker makes less than $32 an hour as a carpenter, he will enter classification code 5403. If he makes $32 an hour or more, he is 5432. The dual-class code for some jobs is that the risk of a claim is lower for a higher-paid skilled worker than a less experienced, lower-paid worker.

Workers' compensation bills you on how much payroll you have for your employees. You may get a rate of $13.50 for a tile contractor, and there is no dual wage for this classification. For every $100 you pay your employee, you will be charged $13.50. If you pay your employee $10,000, you will be charged $1,350 for the employee's worker's compensation insurance.

The classification rates for different trades vary widely. The higher risk of the job, the more expensive the rate is for worker's compensation insurance. Some trades like electrician or drywall have much lower rates than a roofer or a tree trimmer.

It is important to note once you spend a certain amount of money buying workers comp, the WCIRB will issue an experience modification number. This is like a credit score for worker's comp

insurance, which shows your company has experienced claims.

When you're purchasing a new policy, the insurance company will go to the WCIRB to see if you have an experience modification rating to assess your level of risk (minimal-high).

The insured often doesn't know they have an experience modification and may not know they have open claims that their insurance company is paying. This can be an issue when the experience modification goes up by 2/3 from one year to the next. When this happens, the contractor is usually trying to figure out how to afford their worker's comp.

The good news is the claims usually fall off every three years to help lower the rate. It's a lot like having poor credit or points on your driver's license. The WCIRB has a three-year "look back" when creating your experience modification number. Workers' compensation insurance companies all write different types of policies. Some companies don't write roofers or tree trimmers. Many companies don't write contractors because the risk of the work is so high.

It's the insurance broker's job to know what companies will take which trade the contractor is doing. Many contractors think every insurance company is lining up to get their business. But many contractors will have to buy their worker's comp from the state insurance office because they are a new venture or don't have prior coverage to get a loss runs or claims report.

A loss runs report is a report to see if you have any existing claims against you or your business. When getting a quote for worker's comp, you will need a loss runs report issued within 30-60 days from the time you are requesting coverage.

The underwriter wants to see that you don't have any claims on the policy you are looking to replace. Only some insurance companies specialize in writing specific types of risk. The California state law states that you must have worker's comp insurance to hire anyone to work for you. The state demands coverage, so they must provide a place to buy the insurance. In the beginning, private insurance companies don't want to take on new construction companies that don't have a record.

Not all new contractors must buy worker's comp from the state insurance option. It depends on the trade you are doing. It is recommended to ask your broker to ensure you obtain the proper insurance you need from the best source. This chapter provides you with a brief review of insurance related to worker's compensation.

The points I discussed in this chapter will give you insight into how worker's comp benefits both you and your employees. It's also important to know how you will be billed and rated a policy. Your broker should also discuss the WCIRB and the experience modification they issue.

# CHAPTER 5
## BONDING

Bonding is another business expense you will need to purchase before your contractor's license is issued in California. There are two types of bonds. The first type is called a commercial bond or license bond. The state requires this type of bond to protect the consumer if there is an issue. The second type of bond is called a contract bond, also referred to as a bid, performance, or payment bond.

Many people get confused regarding contract bonds and how they work. Consumers attempt to purchase a contract bond to protect them if the contractor doesn't finish the project they hired them to do. However, this is not what contract bonds are for. Contract bonds are set up to protect public works jobs, and sometimes large companies.

If you are doing a job for a city, municipality, or state, they will usually require you to have a bond. This requirement protects the public from losing money if a contractor cannot complete a project. The contractor usually will set up their bonding before bidding on projects. This is because you need to know how much bonding you qualify for.

Contractors often want to start bidding on bigger jobs they don't have experience doing. Typically most contractors have to start bidding on smaller jobs and work their way up to the more significant projects as they get more experience. Bonds are not insurance. They are loans that must be paid back if there is a claim. Many times, people get the bonding confused with insurance. Since a bond must be paid back, you can only get a bond for what you can afford to pay back if there is a claim.

It's similar to obtaining a loan or line of credit. When applying for a bond, the underwriter will go through all the individual's credit, bank statements, financial documents, and project history to verify how much they qualify for. In the beginning, the price for a performance bond is usually about 3% of the bid price.

Contractors often call their insurance broker when they need a bid bond due the next day. But it usually takes about a week to go through the process to set up bonding. The good news is you can generally put up your bid bond. But keep in mind that bid bonds are 10% of your bid amount.

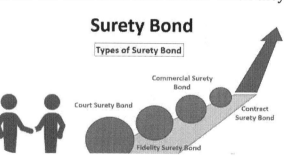

# CHAPTER 6
## COMMERCIAL AUTO

C ommercial auto insurance is another insurance that is commonly required when you're a contractor. Usually, when you are hired to work for a commercial job or as a subcontractor, you will probably be required to have commercial auto insurance. You may be required to have $1,000,000 in coverage and have "Any Auto Coverage." Any Auto Coverage means it will cover any rented and non-owned vehicles for which you may be liable. Not all insurance companies will offer $1,000,000 with Any Auto Coverage. However, many do.

A commercial job might require that level of coverage to protect the company for which you are working. If it's a large commercial company, there's more risk of you having a large claim against them.

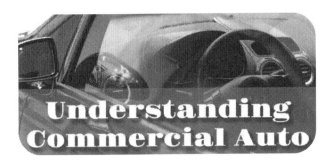

# CHAPTER 7
## EXCESS LIABILITY INSURANCE

A nother product you may be asked to obtain is Excess or Umbrella coverage. This policy will add a more significant amount of insurance if you exhaust your policy's limits. Frequently, this coverage is required when working on commercial projects. When you're hired to work for large companies, they may be concerned that a lawsuit could be more significant than your policy's coverage.

Excess insurance is an umbrella over your general liability auto and workers comp coverage. That's why Excess Insurance is often referred to as Umbrella Insurance. If a claim pays out the total coverage on your policy and doesn't cover the claim amount, the Excess Insurance would then pay out the difference.

### EXCESS LIABILITY VS. UMBRELLA COVERAGE EXPLAINED

**Excess Liability**

Additional insurance coverage that takes effect once limits of a specific underlying insurance policy have been reached.

**Umbrella Coverage**

Provides excess coverage for multiple lines of insurance. Usually more expensive than excess liability since the coverage is more extensive.

# CHAPTER 8
## CERTIFICATES OF INSURANCE

As a contractor, your client will usually ask you for your Certificate of Insurance or (COI). They can and often will ask you to name them as the client on your COI. This is a common request from a contractor, especially if you work on a commercial job. Many policies you purchase will come with a blanket additional insured certificate.

A blanket additional insured endorsement will automatically add your client to the policy without notifying your insurance company. There might be a fee to do this if coverage is not included in your policy. Your client may ask for this since their insurance policy may require them to have it to manage risk for the job.

My clients email me all their COI requests. Sometimes your client might ask to be added to your insurance policy as a scheduled individual. This is pretty common and allows your client to make a claim directly. They will have your policy number and all your insurance information. It's challenging to get this information after the work has been completed, so they usually ask upfront.

# Understanding Your Certificate of Insurance

There are many different additional insured certificates the client can ask for. The following are the ones frequently requested:

**Regular additional certificate -** Used to broaden your coverage over an individual or company that your work could damage.

**Waiver of subrogation certificate** - The waiver of subrogation is the document that stops your insurance company from trying to go after another party to get money for a claim already paid. Let's say you were hurt working as a subcontractor for a general contractor.

Your insurance can go after the general contractor for not having a safe job site and want to be reimbursed for the claim. I would think of this subrogation waiver as giving up your right to be reimbursed for a claim. Often, when a company hires you, and the job involves worker's compensation coverage, the company will ask for a waiver of subrogation certificate because they don't want to get sued if you or your employee gets hurt working on a job.

**Primary non-contributory form and an Ongoing and Completed Operation certificate** are for general liability. Primary non-contributory means that your policy must pay the claim without seeking help from another insurance policy that might be liable.

Ongoing and Completed Operation means that the policy is active during and after the job.

These certificates can be blanket certificates, which means you can use them with all your clients. You can also order these certificates as individual forms with a specific client named. If the forms are not included in your policy, you may have to buy them.

However, sometimes the policy may not allow for additional insured certificates, which is rare. It usually only happens if you're working with a developer or a large general contractor doing track homes, and they have one policy that covers all the subcontractors.

Insurance companies want to stay away from these types of comprehensive WRAP policies since the WRAP policy may want your insurance to cover off-site exposure. If there is a claim, it

**CERTIFICATE OF INSURANCE**

A CERTIFICATE OF INSURANCE IS AN INSURANCE DOCUMENT PROVIDED TO US BY THE VENDOR/CLIENTS INSURANCE CARRIER THE CERTIFICATE WILL LIST THE TYPE OF COVERAGE THAT THE VENDOR/CLIENT MAY HAVE, CARRIER NAME, POLICY LIMITS AND EFFECTIVE DATES

could be significant. In turn, your insurance company may want to avoid a special endorsement for this. Always remember to ask your broker what your policies include or don't include.

# CHAPTER 9
## LAPSES IN COVERAGE & MAKING A CLAIM

L apse in coverage means a "stop" in insurance coverage. Usually, there are two reasons for a lapse or cancellation to occur. Either you have a lapse, and your policy was canceled for non-payment, or secondly, you did not comply with policy requirements during the period. The insurance underwriter usually doesn't want to see a lapse or stop in insurance coverage.

When there is a lapse in coverage, it makes the insured look irresponsible or high risk to insure, and they may not re-write the policy. It is essential never to let your coverage lapse. If you have a claim filed and the insurance company cancels  your policy because you let it lapse, then you could lose coverage for that claim.

You could also lose all prior coverage to all projects completed during that time window for the multiple years the policy was in place. In short, this is a significant problem. It is strongly advised that you never allow your policy to lapse. Also, it is essential to know how to make a claim. Therefore if you are in a position where you must file a claim, things will go smoother.

Often, filing a claim is time-sensitive; the more you know ahead of time, the better. I am writing about this topic because many people are afraid to make a claim. More often than not, people try to handle an issue themselves instead of filing a claim with their insurance company, and the problem worsens, which is common with worker's comp insurance.

What may seem like a simple fix and not a big deal at first may tend to get complicated and unresolved. A frequent example is when an employer says there's no need to file a claim after an injury, and they will pay for someone's medical bills and give them paid time off.

However, if things don't go as initially discussed, the problem lingers for a while or escalates. Later the employee decided to call a lawyer to see what their rights were with the injury. The employer has been sent documents from the employee's lawyer stating that they want more compensation. And then things escalate from there into an expensive court proceeding.

My best professional advice is to make a claim when there seems to be one and get in front of something in the beginning before it turns into a more significant issue that can be hard to manage. The sooner your insurance company's claims adjusters get to the claim, the quicker it can be paid or denied and cost less money and issues. This is the reason you have insurance in the first place!

Another example is when a client called me about two employees who had a fistfight. At first, the employer didn't want to make a claim. He feared his insurance would go up and send the injured employee to the hospital.

Then the employer quickly reconsidered his original decision and decided to call his insurance company to file a claim, which turned out to be a good move by the employer. After receiving care, the employee tried to make a more significant issue out of his injury. The insurance company paid the hospital bill but denied the claim for additional compensation since the employee was treated thoroughly and quickly, and everything was documented.

If the employer hadn't filed the claim and sent the employee to the hospital immediately, it would've been much harder for the insurance company to manage the claim. I haven't seen an issue yet where an insured individual or business regretted making a claim. However, I had seen people who wished to have made a claim before it became a more extensive, complicated, and expensive issue. Always allow your insurance to work for you when it needs to.

Matthew Rogers, CRIS
Insurance Broker
CA Lic.#OK86707
CSLB #1076179
P **(323) 400-6700**
E matt@cisburbank.com
**CIS-Contractors Insurance
Solutions, Inc.
2600 W. Olive Ave. 5th Floor
Burbank, CA 91505**

Made in the USA
Columbia, SC
22 January 2024

30790262R00022